my

whole food

A B C's

written by David Richard

illustrated by Susan Cavaciuti

My Whole Food ABC's

ISBN 1-890612-07-3

Printed in United States of America by Shamrock Graphics.

Vital Health Publishing
P.O. Box 544
Bloomingdale, IL 60108

Toward the health of children,
today and tomorrow.

A is for APPLE
which grows on a tree.

B is for BEETS
for you and for me.

C is for CORN,
all wrapped in a stalk.

D is for DATES,
so sweet and so dark.

E is for EGGS
which are laid by a hen.

F is for FISH
as they dance and swim.

G is for GRAPES,
picked ripe from a vine.

H is for HONEY
on which honeybees dine.

I is for ICEBERG,
a lettuce, you see.

J is for JASMINE,
a kind of green tea.

K is for KIWI,
all fuzzy and brown.

LENTILS

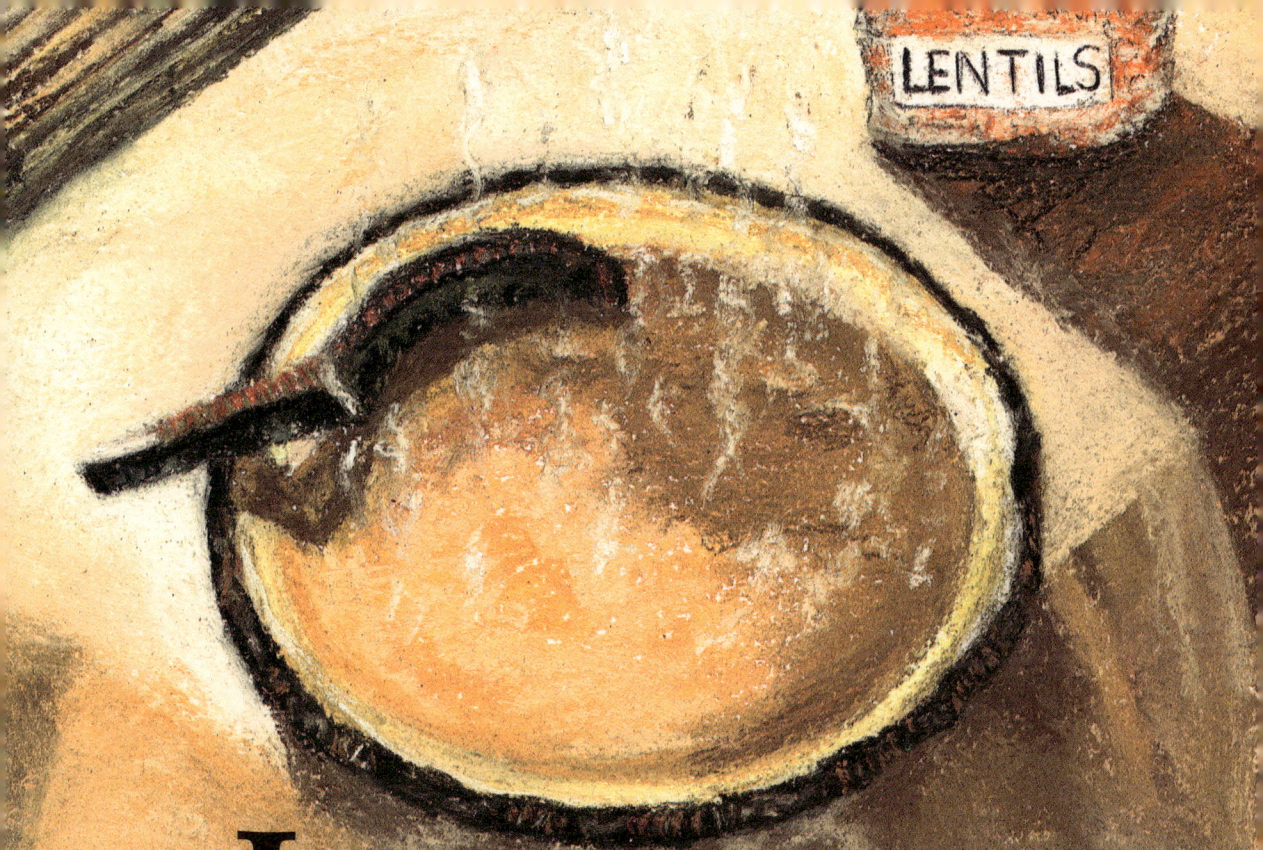

L is for LENTILS;
in soups they are found.

M is for MILLET,
a tiny white grain.

N is for NAVY BEANS
which sailors once named.

O is for ORANGE,
a color <u>and</u> fruit.

P is for PEAS
- green pods are their suit.

Q is for QUINOA
- just try to say that!

(KEEN-WAH)

R is for RICE
to fill up a hat.

S is for SOYBEANS,
all snug in their beds.

T is for TOMATO,
plump, juicy and red.

U is for UME,
a kind of tart plum.

(ŎŎ-ME)

V is for VANILLA
- I'd like to taste some!

W is for WATERMELON,
so juicy and cool.

X is for XMAS PEARS,
decked out for the Yule.

FRESH MILK

NATURAL YOGURT

Y is for YOGURT
from the milk of a cow.

Z is for ZWIEBACK,
a German toast - Wow!

All food from the earth
is abundant in health:

Enjoy it all well
and nourish yourself!